D0963491

Also by Suzanne Lummis

Idiosyncracies (1984)
Falling Short of Heaven (chapbook, 1990)

ANTHOLOGIES:
Stand Up Poetry: The Poetry of Los Angeles and Beyond (co-edited, with Charles Harper Webb, 1990)
Grand Passion: The Poetry of Los Angeles and Beyond (edited, with Charles Harper Webb, 1995)

PLAYS:
October 22, 4004 B.C., Saturday (The Cast Theater, Los Angeles 1987, Seattle 1990)
Night Owls (The Cast Theater, Los Angeles 1989, Houston 1990)

Suzanne Lummis

In DANGER

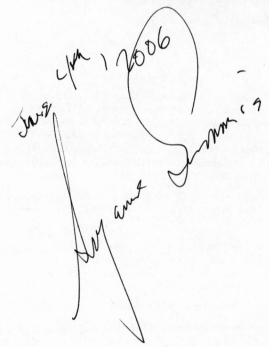

THE ROUNDHOUSE PRESS

For Doug

© 1999 by Suzanne Lummis

All rights reserved. No portion of this work may be reproduced or transmitted in any form or by any means, electronic or mechanical, including photocopying and recording, or by any information storage or retrieval system, without permission in writing from The Roundhouse Press.

Publisher's Cataloging-in-Publication Data
Lummis, Suzanne.
In danger / Suzanne Lummis — 1st ed.
p. cm. — (California poetry series ; v. 2)
ISBN: 0-9666691-1-8 (PBK.)
1. City and town life — California — Los Angeles — Poetry.
2. Los Angeles (Calif.) — Poetry.   I. Title.   II. Series
PS3562.U4687152 1999
811'.54—dc21   99-25604
CIP

Some of the following poems have appeared in *The Antioch Review, The Downtown News, Fourteen Hills: The SFSU Review, The Jacaranda Review, Onthebus, Poetry Flash, Sheila-Na-Gig, Solo, Southern Poetry Review, Pearl,* and the anthologies *Beyond the Valley of the Contemporary Poets, Stand Up Poetry: The Poetry of Los Angeles and Beyond* from Red Wind Books, *Stand Up Poetry: The Anthology* from University Press, Long Beach State University, *Gridlock: Poems of Los Angeles* from Applezabba Press, and in the forthcoming Red Hen Press Anthology. Some of these poems have appeared in the Pennywhistle chapbook, *Falling Short of Heaven.*

Thanks to Terry Kistler for his careful reading of my manuscript, and for the bountiful rewards of his friendship. And thanks to the distinguished photographer Jo Ann Callis for the use of her work.

This is Volume 2 of the California Poetry Series.
Cover Photo: Jo Ann Callis
Author Photo: Gerry Torribio
Cover and Interior Design: David Bullen Design

Distributed to the trade by Consortium Book Sales & Distribution

Subscription orders, inquiries, and correspondence should be addressed to:
California Poetry Series
c/o The Roundhouse Press
P.O. Box 9145
Berkeley, California 94709
phone: 510.549.3564 fax: 510.549.1889
e-mail: roundhouse@heydaybooks.com

Printed in Canada
10   9   8   7   6   5   4   3   2   1

Contents

I.

First the Weather   3
The Man Who Delivers My Paper   4
The Cradle Will Rock   6
No Metamorphosis   7
Writer's Block   9
Outline for Adult Film   11
The Regular Nice Guys   13
Poverty   14
Crash I   15
Why Life is Worth Living   16
Breasts II   18
To the Man in the Parking Lot of Sunset and Normandie   20
Shangri-la   22
Death Rings Marilyn Monroe   24
Past, or Concurrent, Life Memory—with Typo   26

II.

World News   29
Allright Parking   31
The Fahrenheit Chronicles   32

III.

Midnight Special (The Donut Inn)   39
Sea Chanty   41
Letter to My Assailant   42
Graffiti—New York Subway   44
Why Her Name and Face are Everywhere   45
Pomegranates II   47
The Poet's Rancorous Complaint on Her Birthday   50
Gin Alley   52
Death Threats   54
The Barbie Coffin   55
Nicole, Before and After   59

Femme Fatale   *61*

Empty Shell—L.A. '92   *62*

Poem Noir   *63*

Ideas of Heaven   *65*

El Niño, After Visit from Jehovah's Witness   *67*

From the Air   *68*

Electrical Storm, L.A.   *70*

Handwash—Palermo, 1955   *71*

When in Doubt Have a Man Come through the Door
    with a Gun in his Hand   *72*

In DANGER

First the Weather

> Never begin a story with a description of the weather.
> *Donald Barthelme at UCLA lecture*

My house is of brick but something
is blowing it down.
The tenement doors burst
in and windows slam
against the walls of the unrented rooms.
A garbage lid is picked up and flung
with a shock I half love,
and in East Downtown
those who are hungry are cold. Alas,
Barthelme, there is weather in L.A.,
and it insists that it come first.
Up there, in a sky of live wires,
it's the story of our lives tapped out
in a code that's already broken.
So what difference how I begin
or end?
One night on the boulevard
when the sky went electric
like this, I saw Popey's Chicken,
with its clutch of insomniacs
and small spenders,
flare up in cut-throat light.

The Man Who Delivers My Paper

In the half light, while one world
is tearing away from another,
he comes down the hall, laboriously,
as if knee-deep in water.

He leaves at my door the one
gift he can give:
the weather, stock reports,
the death of a stranger,
a child tossed into the rapids,
assassins, rumors,
rumblings in Santiago,
a woman who had one too many,
a man who missed by a hair.

He sets it down gently
as if it were a newborn
or a thing he made with his hands,
like a bomb.

Something passes over my dreams,
dropping its shadow.
He goes with a lighter step than before.
It's as if he's clearing his conscience.
With each paper he leaves
he grows sweeter, more pure.

When I open the door there it is—
indisputably mine.
I could nudge it with my foot
to another door, but what good would that do.
One way or the other
news keeps reaching me.
I could shut myself in, but my phone

would never stop ringing,
voices would whisper their secrets,
their guilty desires.

So I take it in my hands,
unstring and read it,
my catalog of last night's crimes.
You see? Just when you think you've lost
the last of your innocence
you lose more.

The Cradle Will Rock

They fill up the news: dead,
blue as dreaming by the time
they're pulled from the wrecks.
See what happens when the terra firma
goes bad as a bounced check, a promise
broken at both ends? Your body
caves in on you for the last time,
your breath is evicted from your ribcage.
It's Mexico City, '85. Men and women
crawl sobbing over rubble, knock
and knock, but can't get down
to the source of those screams,
and the dying can't come out. Oh who needs
this knowledge cutting close to the bone?!
We fling it away, but each year
scientists chart out more faultlines.
We imagine them under freeways, under
the strung ropes of light we see
from the air—deep
flaws of character running counter
to what we want. They're under our homes.
We sleep above them and are more
amazing than swamis who lie
on platforms of nails. But it happens
in other cities, too, doesn't it—
a sort of feat like flying, a quirk
of evolution, the way humans can know
what they know and still sleep.

No Metamorphosis

In the end they'll lie friendless,
tipped sideways, where
their pinhead hearts stopped.
But, today, out of secret flaws
in the wall, cracks in the master plan,
these blind followings
of instinct come out, low
eaters of what's left behind.
Roaches, it is said, have emotions,
but which ones? No doubt
they're only in awe for a moment,
then it's back to those blunt
bare-handed needs: hunger
and thirst, peewee lust.
They have no memory or sense of time.
At night they think it has always
been night, that this is a dark planet
we live on, missing a sun.
By mid-morning it's as if it's been day
all night, the light always falling
serenely, fluently,
like this to the kitchen floor.
And this is where you come in,
advanced species, up late
as usual and looking for a clean cup.
You are the one who can tell time,
who produces salt water
through ducts and glands,
who reacts to a ringing phone,
You enter and exit with big steps.
In the whole plump
universe,
you are lord of the opposable thumb
and contradictory idea.

You have a life span of 70 years,
time to waste, and these tiny
desires positioned just beyond
getting which must be
followed to the grave. Ah,
but yours will be *marked*.
You might get
a cherub gripping a sprig.

Writer's Block

You dream a man you've never
heard of named Henry Schwinn walks up
and tells you you have no talent.

You wake up with chills
and a hernia in your imagination
knowing he's right.

At 3 a.m. in the winter
on a night of no moon,
who needs such news?

It drives you from bed through the reaches
of cold air to your kitchen, makes you
tear everything out of the cupboard.

You've got to have gin.
You've got to have vodka.
You've got to have crème de banana.

This is your chance
to become the tragic drunk
you've secretly wanted to be.

At last among the pots, chipped ceramics,
scattered barley, and Chiclets
from your trip to New York,

you find a half jar of Kahlua
marked "Merry Christmas, love Bob,
December 31, '81."

What's left of that passion
is sticky as pitch and won't pour.
So you dig down and spoon it trying

to reach China
but reach only the floor,
familiar as your own face.

And when the floor gives way
and you are cradled
and rocked in a body of unnamed water,

you are still not back
in the womb, nor dead,
still not safe,

still not through.
You are still on this planet
not a better one, and still unable

to trade in your own future for some
popular blonde's.
And you still cannot write—

because the broom is no metaphor,
and the percolator will not speak its true name,
and the orange will not open into daylight,

and the hen's eggs are silent,
and the pomegranate is mute.

And when at last the walls start to speak
they sound just like Henry Schwinn.

Outline For Adult Film

As the executive goes down
for the third time,
foam breaks in his hair.
His date rises on a shell.
Her thighs are leopard cubs.
His thighs get super famous.
Her breasts are fundraising
to feed the poor.
His hands make bids and donations.
His lips are vindicated of all lies.
Her lips invent new and better lies.
His balls are bound for glory.

And the postman refuses to let go of the mail.
The housewife keeps punching him;
he keeps deflecting her blows, til
her clothes burst open, then his,
and both sink to their knees—exultant
cries, explosions of postcards
declaring they're fine, sweepstakes,
giddy promotions . . .

And several brides run amuck in the street
and finally into one another's arms,
crying *Yes Yes!* in some remembered tongue.
And they refuse to be coaxed home
by their husbands or mothers
or by public officials.
They refuse to board the plane to Niagara
but roll around in profane embraces,
scoffing at everyone,
their bridal veils flying in a violent wind.

And a secretary is caught off guard
by a vision that was not even scheduled.
As she descends a staircase each
stair turns into arms held out for her.
She rushes down faster.
She believes she is falling in love.
So she rushes down faster.
She believes she'll be caught dishabille—
So she rushes down faster.
She believes the gods look upon her
in particular and say *it is good!*
So she rushes down faster.
She believes she's seized
by her desire. She slips away, it
catches at her again.
So she rushes down faster,
til she forgets everything.
She forgets the past, the infinite,
the impossible. She forgets phone numbers.
She forgets to take notes.
She gets fired!
Broke, on the streets now, she knows
the mystery, hardboiled,
sacrosanct, *The Case of Turning Stairs.*
So she rushes down faster.

The Regular Nice Guys

> We need to meet some new men but there's nobody around
> except all these regular nice guys.
> *a friend*

So you're in this elevator, right?
That's when you spot them,
correct and upright as bowling pins.
No need to consult your guidebook,
you know what they are.
No use trying to escape,
you're surrounded.
No good trying to hide,
this is an elevator.
No use calling for help.
It would be them who would rescue you.

Poverty

It rains.

A stain
　　　appears on my
ceiling
like the map of
a
country people want

out of.

Crash I

Over the traffic, the blast
of sirens, that skid
and crash stood out.
As always, the drivers
were frozen at first
as if they were still
in flight—now
they wander out part-conscious.
A man from one car seeps
a bit from the head.
His passenger throws her arms
around him and cries
as if to make the city
hear. Of course nothing
does but us. All this, the mix
of tears and blood, takes hold,
pulls us down to that deep blue
mood again. We could plunge
from the roof of our fourth
floor now just
for the ornery thrill,
throw it all smack
back in the face of whatever
bright idea
dragged us into this.
Instead we stare, abashed,
unable to move on. We don't
often see it close up
like this: grief,
for once some
stranger's, not our own.

Why Life Is Worth Living

> One could always say that instead
> of the hand grasping the apple
> the hand thrusts the entire
> universe backwards, propelling
> the apple against the hand.
> *The Relativity Explosion*

And here you thought you were ineffectual.
At 2:00 a.m. the pipes of your sink
explode, drowning the air.
You rush in. It's as if water
is walking on water.
And every knob you turn lets go
of another geyser.
Then you know water has rebelled against you.
It will never again lie down,
flat and serviceable.

And when you wear something new
and quite expensive,
a man attacks you with a glass of wine
then apologizes like mad. He'll turn out to be
some worthless stranger
with whom you'll have an affair.

The historians will record that on March 3,
p.m., 1979, across the world
all unfaithful husbands left home
for their new loves,
except your man who went back to his wife.

And when you die you'll be boxed
And shipped to the wrong funeral,
To a gathering where you're recognized
and widely disliked.

And yet, on this dusty unkempt planet,
on which felons have urinated,
on which drunks have vomited for countless years,
there is still one last
unimpeachable glory.

See that ungrasped apple on the kitchen counter?
Let your hand reach.
The Earth slides backwards carrying
a myriad of other planets,
and the sparkling darkness between them,
and tiny lenses of stars,
and great unwieldy suns.

Stand still
and give thanks.
All of space, your life,
all that life is
has brought you this gift. It is fruit
crowning your palm like manna
from some better world.

Breasts II

In my teens they were famous
for their insignificance.
Though I exercised and hoped
beyond hope they remained just figments
of my imagination, or suggestions
of all that is possible—the wealth
that has only half come into this world.

But now in their succinct way
they can hold their own with those
of men's fantasies. Though they don't
drop toward my waist like diving bells,
or precede me when I enter a room,
though they aren't gratuitous
like those featured in *Penthouse,*
they are more elemental,
closer to the heart.

They are endowed with magical properties,
unsounded mysteries.
Like two incipient moons
flattened by darkness
they vanish when I lie on my back.

They are prized by diamond cutters,
vegetarians and collectors of miniatures,
but are shunned by plebeians,
by readers of pulp novels,
and are overlooked by the nearsighted.

Yet a man must not seize them
like mouthfuls of fast food packaged
by lowpaid workers. No!
He must approach them like a man

who was once blind for years
but can now see,
like a man who was alone a long time,
kidnapped by propagandists,
locked up in a room, but is now
free, like a man who has fallen
from his sad and silent past
into my arms and now
everything shines with an almost
unbearable splendor.

As for other poets who've written of their own,
my breasts are indisputably closer
to poetry: precise yet subtle, the most
economical of forms.

In short, my breasts are superior
to all breast poems, to even
(I'm abashed to admit) my own poems.
In this respect I'm in competition with myself
and must strive my whole life
to equal in writing
their exquisitely finite triumph.

To the Man in the Parking Lot of Sunset and Normandie

I was the redhead at the window
of a moving number two bus.
I was trying to open the window
to wave, shout, "How about lunch?"
or, "save me!,"
or, "tell me your dreams!"

You were there with your friend.
You had come to this place
on a motorcycle—not the roughneck kind
with lots of metal and stupid parts.
Yours was designer-sleek, looked
like in good hands it could fly, crash
the back gate of heaven.
You were the one in the black satin jacket
that fit, jeans that fit,
satin-black hair, shoulders,
Hollywood eyes, and who was worth hard cash
just from the waist up.

I was the one on my way
to get my car from the shop.
If I'd had my car I'd have parked it
and run to you like Merle
(Oberon) heading for Larry Olivier.
I'd have said, "I'll make you a star!"
or, "I know my body's not enough,
I'll bring friends!"
And later, calmer, over drinks, I'd say,
"Babe, you're a high-stake game, but I
am the odds-on favorite."
Who cares what it means; I'd say it like
Bacall, look at you as if you were Humphrey.

But the window was jammed. Everyone stared,
first at me then, following my eyes,
at you. The bus took off
with a burst of dirt-flavored smoke
and later I bet some hussy got you,
married you for the good times and bad news.

No good asking what's a heartstop like you
doing in the lot of a Laundromat,
Fast Chicken and 7-Eleven, why
is a gem like me being carried off
in this bus of lost or underpaid souls
to some horrible garage and probably
to some other horrible place after that
without you?

No good saying, "I love you."
It's late, I'm alone.
Who would hear?

Shangri-la

In New York they think all of California is like
L.A. And they think everyone in L.A. has a
maid. And they don't believe you if you try
to tell them.

Radio talk show caller

It's true, here we are all blonde,
even in the dark, on Mondays
or in slow traffic.

Even in our off-guard moments,
startled by a passer-by,
we are young.

Here we are all privileged,
even in our sleep. At night
the maids hover like sweetly

tranquilized angels over
the glazed or enameled surface
of things, purring *clean clean . . .*

It's all true. We girls sip lemon-lime through a straw,
make love, Revlon our nails.
We take our long sleek legs out for a walk,
let them catch light.

When someone snaps, "Get real!"
it hurts us, real pain like we've seen
in the news. So we throw beach robes
over our tans, and cruise down the boulevard
tossing Lifesavers into our mouths,
car radios singing *am.*

New York, is it true
that in the rest of the world it is winter?

Our state is a mosaic of blue pools,
even the Mojave, and the palm trees
line up straight to the Sierra Nevadas,
And the surf comes down slow like
delirious laundry, even near Fresno.

New York, is it true that great cold
makes the bones ache as if broken?

We're sorry we can't be reached
by plane or bus, sorry one can't pull
even the tiniest thing out of a dream.
We're like the landscape inside
a plastic dome filled with water.

But turn us over, then upright.
See?
No snow falls.

Death Rings Marilyn Monroe

On initial reports that she was found
clutching a phone receiver

He was like all the others,
a heavy breather,
but when he called nothing rang.
She touched the receiver to her ear
and heard something like
"Hold me,"
or
"let go."
She thought of telephone lines
crossing the city to the bruised
back streets where litter
drifts on the pavement,
old men shuffle to bed
in fourth-class hotels.
She imagined the last
bar closed, the drunks
snoring in their only shoes,
but one man pressed
into a phone booth.
The night struck him
like a fork musicians use but
he makes no sound
now, dangling
from this wire to a star.

She imagined her body sunk
towards sleep,
        the mystery
of an unhooked phone,
the way
        it purrs.

Then she noticed her own phone,
how it had changed.
All ten numbers read zero.

Baring a satin sheet
she lay down,

the dark mouth at her ear—
her way out,

his way in.

Past, or Concurrent, Life Memory — with Typo

This is how it begins: quotidian
and well after dark.
You're reading the June *Forbes.*
I'm recalling the highlights
of my mid-youth. A kettle steams.
A garaged car pulls out, slow
thought from its cubbyhole.
You turn, *voila,*
a page, and there, in fine
fine print, are you—and for once
you're wrong, those last
terminating
letters of your name transposed. Wee
switches flipped them.
You appear not to notice, but I
look up to see a man whose thoughts
aren't the ones I know, worn
thin from use, a man
who would not answer to his old name.
I believe you will blink this tiny
slip-up away, instead
there's a shift in the letters
that describe your body. At last
something's living inside it.
Like the men who were half goat
you are now half stranger, my contract
with you half betrayal, peril, half
whispered message, late-night
meeting under the clock tower.
Is it the words that pin things down
or me who is coming unhinged? Text
slips from your lap. You rise,
touch me with *ahnds* for *hands,* your body
foreign, versed in victimless

crime, that mistake I let
slide.
I want no
stopping of these dissembling
or disassembling words for things
now. The lamp tipping to the floor
is my intake of breath, my
skin going bare,
                spilled light.
                     Love,
what
is your name and who could speak it
but a timber wolf begging for the moon?

You set
page 11 down on 10. Your mind drops
like a coin between gratings
to the printed page:
Corporate Takeover in Ten Easy Steps.
Yes, that's you in your polo shirt
as I'd know you anywhere,
your fingers on the flowchart
pursuing the well-mapped course.
You give me your favorite look, the one
that implies nothing happened.

Darling, don't raise your eyes
and gaze as if you do
or don't know me. It's all right.
The car is parked, the kettle
lifted from the flame, and no
typographical t
                error broke,
briefly, some transparent page
or membrane between
What Is / What Could Be.

And no one packed her bags, threw
a wisecrack over her shoulder
then set out
in search of a new life.

Part II

World News

It begins with a good opening line.
It begins at a news stand, doesn't it,
where I have just opened a Paris *Vogue*
to the look I don't have, the clothes
I can't buy, the life I will never live.
You come up behind me like the arriving
future, like Fate right on target,
like some ancient prediction
forecast by clairvoyants
come due.

"So . . are you in this issue?"

You robber baron, Man Who Gets Away
With Everything To Start With
Then Comes Back For More,
Man With A Look In Your Eye
give up!
You think I'd go to bed
with a smooth opening line? Well,
maybe I must if you keep
looking like that, like an image
from a calendar, the kind
I'd be embarrassed to buy.

Mr. August, even better than Mr. July,
Mr. Seasons of the Year, Hours
of the Day, and Saturday,
Mr. Night After Night,
Full Moon, O Almanac!
                        Give me your time.

You flavor of all months:
Strawberry, Mocha, Ginger, Rose
King, Garlic King . . . You know,
my life lacks a little something.
Be a pinch of cinnamon.
                              Be salt.

Or let's pick up where we began:
you are the magazine, I the subscriber.
You shall be delivered
unto me. You are the news
of global warmings, bullish
markets and the latest
advance into space.

Or else it is me who is subscribed to
like a good idea.
I am a report of high yields,
a column of opinion; you can read my mind.
Here is the insider news, the lowdown,
the naked truth in pursuit
of a hard fact.

You see, Darling, with your body
and my genius all metaphors become erotic.
O Muse! O great man behind
the great woman, or beneath her . . .
what a team! The way I can't stop talking,
the way you play Man of Few Words. So one
by one, to me,
say them.

Allright Parking

I drive in late, hoping Allright
will make things O.K.
The other cars have pulled out
from between the yellow lines
and gone home. So it's just me,
and my cigarette, and one match
too damp to light. I try
anyway. Meanwhile, the moon
auditions in an empty theater.
An unowned cat crosses the blacktop.
It's too late for anything
that lives to be up, yet it keeps
crossing the divider lines, each
new little space like the last.
If I could slip down and walk
off like that, low,
in the shadows,
in the splendor of dispassion,
I'd leave no I.D.,
my car doors flung
open, my headlights silent
and so bright that in this
terrible place
even the blind could see.

The Fahrenheit Chronicles

i.

Darling, stop me
if you've heard this one before.

When I met you I started dreaming
of fire, but first *The Terrible* kept me awake.
All night the same ambulance fled
past my window filled with critical injuries.
Its red bulbs rotated and boiled. That was August.
So what could I do in that heat-
lit air but roll, toss, like something cornered trying
to round itself out?
I let a sort of fever pass for sleep, but
the bricks of the building got over-baked,
fractured in hairline cracks. Me too, darn,
I'd broken up—puzzle bits that would not
stick. They stood up full height, dark,
foreign women in disarray
They wailed like oracles, mourners or ordinary
victims, women who take exception
to what's taking place.

Later they gathered under my window whispering,
"Don't, don't," but I wanted to be possessed
or lost
and I would listen to no one,
especially me.

ii.

On the second night I dreamt
I was rounding a corner and guessed
I was about to get caught.
There was a shape on the other side, some

criminal set to go for his mark. I froze
like game, but it was only you with
your high opinion of yourself and canceled credit,
you with a card trick in one back
pocket, tiny cross dangling over your heart,
an alibi on the tip of your tongue.
It was you going after my secrets and keeping yours.

It was not you I wanted but climate, Fahrenheit, that altitude
where the air is thin but still holds heat.
I wanted weather and the weather forecast. I

wanted the late-breaking news.
I wanted it delivered to my door. I wanted landscape,
seascape, China and a boat to sail there, a galleon, a whole

fleet, diamonds, steamed milk and honey served to me
on an enamel tray. I wanted to be served.

I wanted to serve Greatness.

I wanted the moon:

the Dark Moon, Medieval, bearer of rumor
and superstition, or the moon in its rarefied
atmosphere partaking of light, the full
Egyptian moon, or the moon that pricks
like a spindle so now I'm under
this spell. All right I wanted you
—your arms, hands, fingers
printed by the New York police.

See, I'm like those other women after all.
I make all the wrong choices.
I'm in love with danger.
I like unhappy endings where no one is spared
but the villain.

You were the B-movie I just had to sit through again

—you lover of warehouses and railroad tracks,
the ticket that exits the city with no
coming back, motels with clothes dropped
on the floor like the thrown-away future,
where the bad art—that broiling
autumnal scene over the bed—won't quit either
in this place where nothing
gives up and sleeps.

Once you came by Greyhound.
The terminal annex littered with smashed-flat
filterless butts was a tip-off.
So like you to appear through the entrance
of the annex nothing recovers from.
Look, the cars jammed on Hope Street can't budge.
Traffic is stuck to the pavement. Everything's
turned hot and stupid in this air and the kind
of love you intend to make to me requires
a cheap room near an alley where forsaken
cats scream at garbage cans they can't
claw their way into.
Why resist?

Only you could make me feel
like this, like the jewel thief's contraband
made off with by a petty crook.

iv.

You leave me at the border, head south
for winter, the bad money riding on you.
You don't wave, don't look back
like Orpheus, but I do—like Mrs. Lot,

Proust, like Grable
looked back from the locker of G.I. Joe.

Now it is you who is dreaming . . .
city of bananas, papayas, fish
basketed in from the nearby sea
and heaped in the marketplace.
I bet they shine like currency you could buy
land with, and a ring for each finger.
Petit conquistador, thief.
You made off with my confessions, but I
confess nothing but lies.

     v.

So like you to pick this wave after wave of
heat to take off.
The newspaper says NO END IN SIGHT.
The sidewalk glitters like sand
men have perished on, and everyone walks
bowed over like lapsed
Christians petitioning to come back,
short order cooks bowing before the baked
air blasted from an open stove.
A few elderly won't rise; faces
have to be covered and carried out.
And one woman sleeps as if dead
then wakes up exhausted.
Though 72% water she burns from the inside.
She takes her temperature.
She takes measure of the situation.
She takes notes.
Her condition is critical.
Ambulances slam down the street
on their way to other traumas.
This all seems familiar,
but worse. The situation

deteriorates. She takes notes.
Her distress is colossal.
She is becoming some kind of statistic.
It's a wonder she is not in the news:
Victim of Circumstance.
She feels like a famine, a ghost town,
a haunted house. She takes notes.
They are the scrawls of a citizen
of a pre-literate culture, Aboriginal,
humid, torn out of dreams . . . uh oh!
She's lost her objectivity, her dry wit!
What will she be without that?
Just an ordinary woman who sits in dim cafeterias
wearing a hat.
She gives up, cashes in, calls it quits, calls it
by its true name. She pays
the ferryman and crosses into melodrama.

Afterward

Anyway, it was just a madness or allergy,
a variation, a little shift away
from the denominator that's most common.
It was a routine forecast on a local station
that became prophecy, fate and its side-effects,
and the same current that sweeps armies
to war swept me to you on that robbed-
blind intersection of some declining city.
And these days?
Nothing is more unknown than your whereabouts.

Darling, don't be smug.
This is a story about me not you, you thing,
utensil, licked stamp, you stage set
in which my dog-eared and disheveled
genius, the still half-illuminated outcast
from some angelic order, could make due.

Whatever we did is gone leaving
a door ajar,
a gate banging in the wind.

You were the flight of stairs I just had
to fling myself down,

the unlit room I entered with nothing
but a struck match.

Part III

Midnight Special (The Donut Inn)

It's late, so the late
Karen Carpenter comes off
the radio at 1 a.m. The diners
complain; she's passé, she's so
post-mortem. You see,
it's Night of the Living.
Outside the sirens rise up
and home in. Now I'm upstairs
asleep, lost to this din,
but downstairs the Usuals
stake out a square
of linoleum, sit down and
fit in.

Like the jailed I bet
they get the same damn thing.
Some special—Styrofoam.
They sip the rim. I bet
at this hour the donuts
lie face up, half
human. The walls are glass
there, so those guys can see
the fix they're in: a block
of illegally parked cars,
laundries, liquor stores with
something for everyone who still
can't win.

At a time like this who
drinks caffeine with cream

or black? They must have given
up. They must know
they won't sleep again. I bet
when Macbeth set out
to kill it he thought, well,
here's someplace to begin.
I may be asleep, but my insomniac
heart rides out to join up
with them, those late,
late bloomers at
The Donut Inn.

Sea Chanty

San Francisco

What winds around your feet
is the shade of tarnished
armor, cold. A cramp
shoots up your bones, drives
you out, like tacks. Out
there, the bulky mass sounds
along its floor. Over
your head, deep, cold. If
you wade out your heart
might crack, you
think. It's smell is salt,
feral, both cold and hot.
You let it burn you white,
sole of foot, of palm, your
heart will snap. It goes like
this: we love the sea, it
doesn't love us back.

Letter to My Assailant

On such occasions
one comes to know someone spectacularly fast.
Even with your unfriendly arm at my throat
you could hide nothing from me.
Your failures with women, for instance,
filed through my mind.
And I knew your father was hostile to doors.
He liked to slam them or break them down.
Your mother worked her way up from dimestore
to drugstore. Even in her grave
her hopes kept shrinking.
Now she's thin as a spindle.
I even knew without looking
your socks had red diamonds
like a small town boy's. In fact,
with my breath stopped in my throat
your whole life flashed past my eyes,
but I didn't let on.
"I can't breathe," I gasped,
and you loosened your hold.
I suppose I should have been grateful,
instead I felt impatient with men,
with their small favors.
I suppose you felt the same about me.
You'd no sooner reached through my torn blouse
when my screams made you bolt.
We leapt from each other
like two hares released from a trap. Oh, oh,
something's not right between men and women.
Perhaps we talked too much,
or did we leave too much unsaid?
When you ripped my shirt mumbling
"I don't want to hurt you,"
I replied, "That's what they all say."

I'll admit I was glib if you'll admit
you were insensitive. Look,
the world is brimming with happy couples,
benign marriages, with men and women
who've adjusted to each other's defects.
Couldn't we adjust to each other's defects?
I'll begin by trying harder not to forget you,
to remember more clearly
your approximate height, your brown shirt
which I described to the police.
Our encounter must stand out in our minds,
distinct from all others.
I never intended
all this to become blurred in my memory,
to confuse you with other men.

Graffiti — New York Subway

He began with words,
but the letters broke down.
He tried to wind them back up.
He tried to catch hold,
looping and circling.
He tried to change the whites
of these walls to blood
red and blood black, then ignite
this car, its passengers,
with nothing but pure emotion.
That's never enough.
He made strings of holes,
then, a net;
things won't escape.
It leaves an imprint on your
mind's eye you can't blink off.
Now
the J train's headed
for some private nightmare—
you missed your stop—
and the guy who scribbled
all this one night in a
fever of cast away
faith, or whatever
that is unraveling its
burnt ends, walks
somewhere with no
change in his pocket,
no future,
owning nothing but you.

Why Her Name and Face Are Everywhere

On the West side the palms
line up straight along
Boulevards and head
for the sea, but even there
the air looks bleached as if
heat had scorched the color out.

The bends and turns of the Harbor
Freeway enter Downtown's
tall buildings. Small cars
are hunting for shade. They say
the next quake will pop
the plate glass VP's gaze

down from, bury these streets
under ten feet of shards. Imagine
the reflected sun, the great
shine. Imagine the future.
In the East side's Egg
'n' Burger shacks dark

bodies hunch up, touch
those old lotto stubs in their pockets,
washed soft and unlucky. One pulls
a kingsize from its pack
and smokes in this heat. He's small
but leans back heavily

and tries not to think. And the video
game lights keep blinking at
full noon. Traffic shines.
Diesel fumes burst
out black, blossom, then vanish
up. God we

need a charm for this
city, a name like a prayer
to save us. Be alchemy that changes
base metal to gold. Be cool
like water. Do it—make
the real less real, Marilyn

Monroe.

Pomegranates II

i. Fairy Tale Ends / The Love Poem

It's meant to stay shut
and dark as
      Bluebeard's closet,
but I've opened mine. Now
this round of blood cells won't close.
These are the reds of admissible evidence
and enough guilt to feed everyone. Good, let's
start washing our hands like Macbeth's wife. Why,
the air from our palms might
rise, leave its tincture on heaven. Who
knows? But it's our fault we got lost.
At the end of this road someone gets baked
in a clay oven. Did you imagine
we'd ever get back?
                   Darling,
if one of us tossed these seeds behind us
like drops
  from
      the wounded
the other would peck them away.

ii. Encyclopedia: The Disaster Poem

The Red Sea stretches from the Suez
to the Gulf of Aden.
In color that deep one could drown.

Red sands are coated with iron oxide and found
only in arid climates,
           in heat waves

rising like prayers that almost
reach the ear of God.

Red rain dropped near Java. First,
Krakatoa took an island
of little villages, smoothed them
with its hand of lava, its hand of endings
and new beginnings. The dust
finally settled on the dust, but
the next rain fell down
red on Central Asia, factory-red
like water soiled by chemicals,
smeared by fire.
People ran to their homes,
locked their doors, but it pooled
through ceilings—the dead
come unburied from heaven,
the losses that find their way back.

      Because their cool
effulgent, flung-
   down glamour captures
your eye, that is,
     takes it captive,
you start to slide
 the strung pearls
  from the dresser top
   when it begins
 to open—
       the door.
Red Handed:
one of the many ways to be caught.

iii. Exorcism: The Incantatory Poem

You fabulous breaking heart, cheap
sideshow attraction, you locked
box sprung wide spilling pieces
of alphabets spelling out trouble,
you injury in a world of so many,
go, for once be something escap-
ing through an open door. Get
lost.

The Poet's Rancorous Complaint on Her Birthday

> One of these men who can be a car salesman
> or a tourist from Syracuse or a hired assassin.
> *John MacDonald via Donald Justice*

I'm one of those women
who could've been the target of some
sting operation and the brains behind it.
Picture me designing my own
end, placing the decoys, the hitmen,
then sealing my routes of escape.
Later they'd say it was that dark
twist in my genius, self against
self, that shut down my reign — pride
of the demimonde, sultana
of the near-victimless crime.
Or
I might have worked the late-shift
at a diner near Kansas City. I'd refuse to take orders.
I'd come to your table
and you'd have to take mine.
Ask how I survived I'd say
it was some fast talking
got me this far, and a '67 Corvette.
Or that could be me on the run
from my husband, with all I can carry
in a Macy's bag, cosmetics case and one
hat box, catching the next bus out.
You could take the seat next to mine.
You could be a locksmith, barkeep
or private eye. You could pass
for a tourist from Syracuse
with your new minted ID and a shine
on each shoe. You could be wanted,
and I wanted by you.
We could be the pair in the summer's

big budget movie, one where shots
get fired but everyone winds up
with the person they love.
It'd be a 10-cylinder diesel
that carried me there,
and that road opening out to adventure.
Or I could be less benign than you think,
with my hat box, white gloves.
I could be a woman with a motive,
a guarded secret. If that guard
goes down nothing will explain
what happens next, thriller
turns that leave the man who plucked
this paperback from the bin marked
"two for one" on the side of a road
holding his tassled bookmark
while I go on alone.
And when these stories came full
circle I'd be back at my own radiant,
dangerous origin, choices winking
like the city at night taken in
from a top floor suite.
Or
I could have been anyone
who would never have allowed this,
let poetry dump her off here:
September 13, 1991, forty, broke, half-
sober, with a flu coming on,
in the Apartment House of Faded Glory,

on the street of sirens and sprung alarms.

Gin Alley

The women who enter there find nothing
but desperation and lust to drink.
cover blurb from old pulp novel

It's 1939, a Monday, and a Depression.
So me I fasten one tall heel the color
of heart's blood on each foot
and go to Gin Alley.
I'm not thirsty tonight,
desperation and lust will do fine.

Inside another tall heel catches my eye.
His silk shirt looks like it's been
hand-washed by some
dye-job blonde. It's got three
open buttons, three closed, and the last
tucked away in the realm of the imagination.
Something about him makes me
slip a thin cigarette in my mouth
and start tapping my bullet shaped nails.
When he catches my drift he walks
his arms and legs over my way
and says something witty like, "Hi."

I take a smooth sip from a lousy year.
I say, "Not yet but I'm getting there."

He says, "You look lonely. I can fix that."

I say, "I'm short a buck for a fifth.
Can you fix that too?"

He says, "Oh, hard luck case, huh?"

I give him the kind of look
that makes a man feel needed.

"Yeah, so let's hope you're good for
a half night of hard luck."

Then, in the middle of page 24 three big things
happen at the same time: 1) the bar man smacks
down a glass of bad tap water and bad gin;
2) the dreamboat locks onto me like heavy machinery;
and 3) you, the page-turner, decide I'm a tramp.

Yeah? Listen, Joe, the only one around here worse
off than me is you, the loser who's reading this book.
At least I get to jump this hayride on page 236,
but you'll sail right past it and keep on going
—probably to the corner diner where you'll perch
round-shouldered—Mr. Small Change and Big Dreams,
with a fry stain on his lapel. It's the real world
you're in, kid, where no one's quite good enough
to wisecrack their way through.

Death Threats

2 a.m. and this caller's hooked
on pure reaction, but death
is old news, not worth phoning in.
All night I hear sirens
get off to a start too

late to save anyone. I
disconnect, leave him
holding the receiver like
a handle that was just
torn off. Go out,

stranger,
to your little table
with the crumpled napkins,
the meltdown

of shot glass ice, small,

small change. Sit
in the scent of women, the drift
of their cigarettes,
these lives unavailable, like
points of light who

drive past. Be
no one specific: the regular
who tips cheap, stays too late,
till the waitresses
wish he'd get off his ass and go.

The Barbie Coffin

When Barbie realizes the price for that brief
indiscretion near the high school gym lockers
during her one-year reunion, she sets out to shop.

She doesn't return this time in her flash
pink coupe, the top flung breezily down,
Neiman Marcus bags piled in the seats like
bounty from a tiny god, but in a huge rental truck.

Her mom, of whom we know little, of whom
even Barbie knows little, wails
at the unloading of oblong crates,
"Barbie, the garage, the entire backyard
are crammed full—your golf cart,
dune buggy, your Victorian carriage and horse,
the portable reflecting pond with the rose
flood lamps and little motorized swans!
And now all these coffins? Honey,
you'd look fine in a nice urn."

Barbie has charged the rosewood casket
with quilted pink satin interior
and full length mirror;
the Queen-size with Baroque-style trim
and cupid motif, and a tape
that plays non-stop: "Girl from Ipanema"
and selections from Maya Angelou;
and the "health-conscious" model
that pumps in fresh air.

But which one to pick, and what to wear?
She contemplates death, the hard facts:
bodies trapped in outdated styles,
in granny dresses from '66,

in the glitter glam look from '72,
and those unfortunate girls who died in '96,
trudging to eternity in men's shoes.
Terrible to live forever
with a single choice ...
well, not *live*
exactly.

She sinks into a mood, odd,
unfitting, like nothing she felt as
Tahitian Barbie, Career Girl, Civil War Barbie.
She discovers Plath, gets her
on the deepest level—that line she wrote
on her last day, when the mid-winter freeze
bit the walls of her walk-up flat:
The dead woman is perfected ...

The phone rings,
rings, like the bell that tolls for thee
and thee thinks Barbie—it's Ken. She does
not answer, lets him hang like a figurine
in the rinse of her benign indifference, wash
of dry light. She is reading Camus. She is way
into Joan Didion.

Meanwhile, back at the toy works,
the VP's who track the life
of the teen doll spot a new opportunity.
The world has changed, it's ready for
Depressive Barbie!
No, kids won't get that ... Bummed Barbie!
No, too negative ... Complicated Barbie,
with her medicine cabinet that snaps
open with a sound like a tongue click,
shelves stocked with colorful pills,
one for each thing that goes wrong.

But Barbie no longer cares about merchandise,
the things of this world.
She is reading St. John of the Cross,
the poems conjured in his delirium,
locked in a 6 x 10 cell, light shut out
on all sides, except for high on the wall,
one slot. He
could see them, the ghosts of his up-stretched hands.

If you want to possess everything
You must desire to possess nothing.

If you wish to arrive at that which you possess not
You must go by a way which you possess not.

For in order to proceed from all things to the All
You must deny yourself wholly in all things.

Meanwhile, in the land beyond Never Never,
in the Land of Plenty and Right Now,
the VP's applaud their next idea—
Long Dark Night of the Soul Barbie
with her colorful, compact cell.
They love the one slot concept;
it can double as a little bank.

Barbie doesn't hear them, or care.
She is fasting. She is dreaming.
She is drinking from the cup of the spirit. .
She has given to the poor her prom dress,
her racks of high heels,
her entire tennis ensemble, and moved
to East Downtown L.A.

     HOT AND COLD RUNNING WATER
     LOW WEEKLY RATES

Who can explain this odd transformation?
Not Ken, who is drowning his grief at the golf course
and in calls to a popular therapist on 90 fm,
but he does have a theory:
"She was O.K. with the fatal disease,
but things went weird when she got into poetry."

Barbie is buried, as she asked, in a smock
of dark muslin, a cobble stone marking the spot.
Dead, she is smiling in a new way,
mysterious, secretive, almost celestial,
a smile that pleases no one but her.

The VP's are dejected at first;
the untimely death of their product
nosedives company stock, until together
they brainstorm her come-back.
This will be the biggest toy ever, beyond
hoola hoops, beyond cabbage patch dolls!

That Christmas
in three-bedroom suites with river views,
in projects nestled next to the waste plants,
in flaking hot bungalows with trapped-in flies,
across America, she is wrapped, wrapped,
placed under trees.

Living Dead Barbie
comes with a colorful grave to rise out of. Now
she's an even more focused consumer—got
her eye on your spendthrift heart. And oh,
those too-cool rags, that pale Goth look,
will draw you in like a white sale.
She's so gorgeous, so awesome, so totally perfect, it's
scary.

Nicole, Before and After

Nicole and I shared a dream. We
wanted to stop being male dependent,
give up alcohol and drugs and open up
a Starbucks coffee house.

According to Resnick Nicole felt only
penetration qualified as cheating.

We called them the Starbucks boys.

From Los Angeles Times review of Faye Resnick's book, Nicole, (1/22/95)

i.

We'll start with Kenyan,
French Roast and Pistachio,
wind up with Leroy, Pierre,
and Ignacio. It's not
cheating, just fellatio.
And there will be time
to hit a mall,
time for drugs and alcohol.
To sleep this off
I've got Nembutal.
Or else I, you know,
maybe could
stick with Oranthol
and sleep for good.

ii.

I wasn't perfect,
but he was deranged—
since I got murdered,
though, I've really changed.
But some men don't get it
especially O.J.,
still messing around

on the green all day.
I'd rather be me
than him— *Por que?*
'Cause mine poured from me,
his sorry life
just drips away.
But I miss those Star
struck boys—and, Hey,
kiss them for me
will you, Faye.

Femme Fatale

It's a crime story she's in:
betrayal and larceny, few clues.
Someone stole what she lived for,
made off like a thief in the night
or high noon. What shall she do?
Put a heel on each foot and set out,
making a snapping sound as she steps.
The man she loves smiles
from the drugstore's rack
of magazines, just in.
Looks like he's wrapped his movie,
dropped his wife on a Frisian Island
and is flying his girlfriend to St. Tropez.
The men who love her finger coins
in the stale linings of their front
pockets and whimper *What's your name?*
The job she wanted went
to the man who tells the truth
from one side of his mouth, lies
from the other: a bilingual.
The job she got lets her
answer the questioning phone all day.
Her disappointment has appetite,
gravity. Fall in, you'll be crunched
and munched, stretched
thin as Fettuccine. Watch out for her,
this woman, there is more than one.
That woman with you, for instance,
checking herself in the mirror
to see where she stands—
she's innocent so far, but someone
will disappoint her.
Even now you're beginning to.
Even now you're in danger.

Empty Shell — L.A. '92

I don't like the smell it leaves
on my fingers, dumb brass
worthless as the husk from corn,
shuck of bean, skin the snake
gets rid of. This is no eggshell,
though someone did break
into flesh and bone. Too late
for the cavalry to ride in now, king's
horses, king's men. Look at it,
just a bit more of the miscellany
that makes up the world, useless.
I can't put it to my ear and hear the sea;
the thing won't deliver — no history
worth hawking. It didn't kill what-
was-his-name? at the corner of Vermont
and Santa Monica where Payless Shoes
burned all night on TV. The bullet
did that, the gun, the finger
on the trigger did it, the man
pulling the trigger, the man's mind, his
failed life did it. Hell,
poets, who cares about our tiny
productions congratulating ourselves
on our sincerity and deep-felt feelings?
Who cares about our swell-headed sermons?
Friends, we've gazed upon the heart
of darkness steaming in a raw heat, a lump
no dog would gnaw on, and our poems
failed us. We failed our poems. This one,
see, peers into a small burnt hole
in itself it can't fill, then
comes to a bad end.

Poem Noir

Light rakes
across my window
with that sound we call *chop*
chop, then circles back. It's
keeping the place under wraps,
winding, winding, in a sticky
thread, the bad and the good.
Seems someone used a gun
in a crime again, then
ran home.
And last night cries
from the street, so
I looked out. But it was empty—
hell—just beat-down rain, bunkers
of concrete lodged like crude
ships that sank, and the bulb-
lit sign GOOD WILL.
But whenever I've been mugged
it wasn't here—near
Fairfax once. The gun
against my head made a tiny
pricking sound like a watch,
or like a click
inside a watch, that pin
drop we can't hear
between the tick
and the tock. It burnt
my imagination, woke it up.
But I've got stories worse
than that. Two assholes
dragged me off the street.
Like I'd have seen them
coming, right? But
I was checking my make-up

under a light.
What went down (this
rhymes) was not a pretty sight.
There's things I can't
tell, even in poetry, you
understand that? Anyway,
so what. A cool beam
sweeps into my room
then circles up.
But I was born in '51, see,
that far back, and still
no cop's had to trace
in dimestore chalk
the outline of my shape
where I stopped, leaned
forward, not
because I'd spotted
my name in cement. Then
knelt on
one knee, not
because I was searching
for something I'd lost.
Then two,
not because I was praying.
Then sat,
not because I was suddenly
tired of all this.
Then lay.

Ideas of Heaven

I.

The walls there are shell white.
There are bowls of goldfish,
$\qquad\qquad$ rain water.

$\qquad$ Blue azaleas in a white vase.

Or are they white lilies
in a blue vase, a vase of blue
marble with traces of gold
so faint it may be
$\qquad\qquad$ imagination?

Suddenly the fish are tropical,
half wild, little jewels
that light up at night,
inextinguishable
$\qquad\qquad$ fairground lights.

The walls are still white.
It's day again.
There's a breeze in the curtains,
a bay window opening upon sea
and lighthouse or
$\qquad\qquad$ far hills.
You have
only to think of it,

an unfolding green landscape,
Renaissance perspective,
horses silhouetted in a fine mist.
See straight through it,
the penetrating clear air, till

someone rides bareback
in the distant woods.

No,
it's not distant, this
enchanted forest where you may
open your eyes
as a child, spellbound
and dream-blown, struck
                           by wonder.

          ii.

What do people do there in heaven?

We don't know.

We are far off from knowing.

But you don't stop being happy in heaven
even when you cry.

Your tears pool in your cupped palms
and light the way home.

El Niño, After Visit from Jehovah's Witness

And so he who vowed
to come like a thief comes
like this, a pinging on the roof's
tin spot, hose-like
gushing from roof
to drenched ground,
currents in the street, in
my room—drip, then . . .
drip. He
who said he'd come
by fire next time
lied. My frail iceland
poppies head down,
drowned, the ocean's
heated patch, a burn
from somewhere pointed
toward my chest—heaven
lies. In bed I curl up. An old
anger and fright kicks
in its nailed down crate.
L.A. West, grand homes
dislodge from the mud,
foundations split. A piece
in my head is in danger
of prying loose.
Even dry my soul
and I felt lost,
but we should have guessed.
The second coming comes
drop by drop
as the sea hums and rocks
its newborn part:
body of water,
hot heart.

From the Air

Hunger can't live
in that beadwork needled
by electric light my
plane sinks towards as if
heaven is not above
us but below, a
hard thin heaven.
Ambers, points
of aquamarine make pin-
holes in my lung or
heart, like a type of love.
When I step from the plane
I'll be snuffed, flesh
smoked by voltage,
self sucked into a jewel.
Alien genius made that
continent down there,
flushed with the radioactive.
What could walk
upright in this field?
Their beauty lies
in their bodies burning
like red ants against
the cold, eyes
celled like a fly's.
Or else they wear
the same mask
of human flesh as I.
Like them I'll enter
my car, snap shut
the door, be pulled
to the fast lane
of the 101, the 10, bulb
of lit-up air sent

down a vein, then
break off and farther
off, drop
to the shadowy back
streets of bullet-holed
lights. Nothing
in vacated heaven crossed
by spies can look
down on me now,
in this deep
anonymous darkness
that belongs to me.

Electrical Storm, L.A.

City of sirens and lowdown ways, neons
wincing like nerve ends, see
what you've done?
                              —budged
or burnt them, woken
the old gods
up. The sky messengers
their voltage,
                    fallout
          of burst code. And
something restless in me, it
feels like a ship flung
                              up
and down hard
by deep water, sends
out its sonar and there is
                              an answering.
                    So don't
call it "rain," she who comes
down like words for hunger
like ways to cry thief.
                              Love,
it's the whack
of language we can't

come undrowned in now.

Handwash — Palermo, 1955

Those steep raked steps
were stone and dropped
below the street. The white
dark down there
was clean. Strong armed
women heaved the lumps
of sheets. Hell
didn't smoke, it steamed.
My mother took
my hand and coaxed, "What's wrong?"
The streets smelled like sea
and garlic, potted blooms.
The windowsills were painted
red and blue. I loved
the surface world.
Down there, damp flesh and iron,
iron slabs. When cloth
was pressed it hissed. Shapes
of air burst up, so fierce,
so unrehearsed. Down there
muscled arms made clothes
too hot to wear. They'd make me
flat and lambent like the moon.
I dug in my feet, hung on,
but I was aimed, anyway, straight
toward the unknown. Who knew then?
My mother worried, "Susie,
what is wrong?" then took
the laundry down alone.

When In Doubt Have a Man Come Through the Door with a Gun in His Hand

Raymond Chandler via Lawrence Raab

I'm in doubt, all right, let's
lock the door, dear, lest
a gun come through in a hand

attached to some punk,
some goofball declaring it's all
the fault of society. Or is it

you who comes through the door
shouting gibberish, how I
doubted your word,

how I pretended but never believed . . .
"Lies! Lies!" The syllable yelps
make me think of a man detached

from his ski party calling
for help, but now I'm not sure
who cried "Lies!" I had thought

it was you, but then why
am I framed in this doorway, this
stunned .22 in my hand

weeping a curl of smoke?
And who was it again I just
blasted straight out of this fiction,

this construct of lies? Dear,
if you're still here fetch me
some aspirin and a stiff drink,

I have a headache. It's not
the suspense that's killing me,
it's that existentialist doubt—

I got those unreality blues.
If only I could arrange
for the right man to come

through the door with a gun . . . or,
no, not a gun . . . a fruit
and cheese basket, singing

telegram? A package stuffed
with hard cash, laundered
and pressed with an iron?

I'm certain only of the door.
Yes, there is always
a door, in fairy tales the portal

to a different world. But here
its "knock knock" is the set-up
of an old joke, or the question

that might turn out to be loaded.
Or, like the sound of one
conferring with oneself, it might

just echo back

Who's there?

VOLUME 1: *One Hand on the Wheel* by Dan Bellm
VOLUME 2: *In Danger* by Suzanne Lummis
VOLUME 3: *The Dumbbell Nebula* by Steve Kowit
VOLUME 4: *Listening to Winter* by Molly Fisk

The *California Poetry Series* celebrates the great diversity of aesthetics, culture, geography, and ethnicity of the state by publishing work by poets with strong ties to California. Books within this series are published quarterly and feature the work of a single poet, or in some cases two or more poets with a clear affinity. Malcolm Margolin of Heyday Books is publisher; Joyce Jenkins of Poetry Flash is editor.

An advisory board of prominent poets and other cultural leaders has been assembled to help support the series. These include Alfred Arteaga, Chana Bloch, Christopher Buckley, Marilyn Chin, Karen Clark, Wanda Coleman, Gillian Conoley, Peter Coyote, Jim Dodge, Lawrence Ferlinghetti, Jack Foley, Jewelle Gomez, Robert Hass, Jane Hirshfield, Fanny Howe, Lawson Inada, Jaime Jacinto, Diem Jones, Stephen Kessler, William Kistler, Carolyn Kizer, Steve Kowit, Dorianne Laux, Philip Levine, Genny Lim, Suzanne Lummis, Lewis MacAdams, David Mas Masumoto, David Meltzer, Deena Metzger, Carol Muske, Jim Paul, Kay Ryan, Richard Silberg, Gary Snyder, Dr. Kevin Starr, David St. John, Sedge Thomson, Alan Williamson, and Gary Young.

Books in the *California Poetry Series* are available at bookstores nationwide or by subscription. For more information contact:
California Poetry Series
c/o The Roundhouse Press
P.O. Box 9145
Berkeley, California 94709
phone: 510.549.3564   fax: 510.549.1889
e-mail: roundhouse@heydaybooks.com